DANGEROUS MAMMALS

BEARS

Madison Parker

NorwoodHouse Press

Library of Congress Cataloging-in-Publication Data:

Names: Parker, Madison.
Title: Bears / Madison Parker.
Description: Buffalo, NY : Norwood House Press, 2025. | Series: Dangerous mammals | Includes glossary and index.
Identifiers: ISBN 9781684502592 (pbk.) | ISBN 9781684502608 (library bound) | ISBN 9781684502615 (ebook)
Subjects: LCSH: Bears--Juvenile literature. | Bears--Behavior--Juvenile literature.
Classification: LCC QL737.C27 P375 2025 | DDC 599.78--dc23

Published in 2025 by
Norwood House Press
2544 Clinton Street
Buffalo, NY 14224

Designer: Ocean Books
Editor: Kim Thompson

Photo credits: Cover, p. 1 Spirit9/Shutterstock.com; pp. 5, 21 Sergey Uryadnikov/Shutterstock.com; p. 6 Vaciav Sebek/Shutterstock.com; p. 7 Scott E Read/Shutterstock.com; p. 11 Fernan Archilla/Shutterstock.com; p. 12 Yatra4289/Shutterstock.com; p. 13 Gangadhar A G; p. 14 Akkharat Jarusilawong/Shutterstock.com; p. 17 Martin Rudlop Photography/Shutterstock.com; p. 18 Miroslav Chytil/Shutterstock.com; p. 21 MPH Photos/Shutterstock.com

Printed in the United States of America

Some of the images in this book illustrate individuals who are models. The depictions do not imply actual situations or events.

CPSIA compliance information: Batch #CW25NHP: For further information contact Norwood House Press at 1-800-237-9932.

TABLE OF CONTENTS

MEET THE BEAR

Bears are big, furry animals. They are **mammals**, just like humans! They feed milk to their babies.

TYPES OF BEARS

Polar bears live near Earth's North Pole. If people enter their **territory**, they might chase or try to bite.

Grizzly bears live in North America's forests and mountains. When they feel **threatened**, they might roar, **charge**, or slap with their big paws.

Black bears live in North America's forests. They can be dangerous if they find food near people. They might **ransack** cars looking for treats.

Giant pandas are bears that live in China's **bamboo** forests. They are usually not dangerous, but they will bite if they are scared or if they get surprised.

Spectacled bears have light fur on their faces. They live in South America's mountains. They are shy, but they may scratch or bite if they feel trapped.

Sun bears are small bears with a golden chest patch. They live in Southeast Asia's forests. They are not usually dangerous. If they feel threatened, they might **nip** or claw.

Sloth bears live in India's forests. They do not usually bother people. When they are protecting their babies, they might charge or swipe with their claws.

FAVORITE FOODS

Bears eat foods they find in their **habitats**. Giant pandas eat lots of bamboo. They use their strong teeth to chew it.

Polar bears are good hunters. They wait by the ice to catch seals coming in and out of the water.

Grizzly bears eat berries and plants from the forest. They catch fish in rivers and streams.

STAYING SAFE AROUND BEARS

If you see a bear, do not run. Running can make the bear chase you. Try to make your body look big. Keep looking at the bear as you slowly move away.

Bears like to eat what you eat, so keep your food away from them. If you are outside, put it up high in a safe spot so bears cannot get it.

If a bear comes close, do not touch it. Stay calm. Get help from a grown-up or go to a safe place. Remember, bears usually do not want to hurt you.

GLOSSARY

bamboo (bam-BOO): a tropical plant that has a hollow, woody stem

charge (chahrj): to attack in a rush

habitats (HAB-i-tats): places where animals are usually found; places where animals can find what they need to survive

mammals (MAM-uhlz): animals that are warm-blooded, that have hair or fur, that usually give birth to live babies, and that produce milk to feed their babies

nip (nip): to bite quickly but not firmly

ransack (RAN-sak): to search a place violently, usually looking for things to steal

territory (TER-i-tor-ee): an area that is occupied and defended by an animal and that often contains the animal's nest, den, or home

threatened (THRE-tuhnd): in danger of being harmed

THINKING QUESTIONS

1. Why are bears mammals?
2. What kinds of food do bears like to eat?
3. What should you do if you see a bear?
4. How are polar bears and sun bears alike and different?
5. Where do bears live?

INDEX

ABOUT THE AUTHOR

Madison Parker spent her childhood in the city of Chicago, Illinois. A farm girl at heart, today she lives in Wisconsin with her husband and four children on a small farm with cows, goats, chickens, and two miniature horses named Harley and David. Her favorite dessert is vanilla frozen custard with rainbow sprinkles, even in the winter.